SCHOLASTIC

FRACTIONS
PRACTICE PUZZLES

40 Reproducible Solve-the-Riddle Activity Pages
That Help All Kids Master Fractions

by Bob Hugel

NEW YORK • TORONTO • LONDON • AUCKLAND • SYDNEY
MEXICO CITY • NEW DELHI • HONG KONG • BUENOS AIRES

Teaching Resources

Dedication

To Dana, my favorite girl

Cover design by Maria Lilja
Cover illustration by Kelly Kennedy
Interior design by Holly Grundon
Interior illustrations by Mike Moran

ISBN 0-439-51377-4
Copyright © 2005 by Bob Hugel
All rights reserved.
Printed in the U.S.A.

7 8 9 10   40   21 20 19 18 17 16 15 14 13

Contents

Introduction

Welcome to *FunnyBone Books: Fractions Practice Puzzles*, a surefire way to get students excited about math. This book combines basic fraction problems with loads of hilarious riddles guaranteed to get students revved up for learning.

As you may know, one of the keys to helping students learn successfully is to make learning fun. That's why each page of *Fractions Practice Puzzles* starts with an amusing riddle. Your students will be motivated to solve the fractions problems because the answers will help them find the rib-tickling solution to each riddle.

Along the way, your students will be drilled on several fraction skills, including adding, subtracting, multiplying, and dividing fractions, computing with mixed numbers, simplifying fractions, and solving fraction word problems. We hope your students enjoy *Fractions Practice Puzzles* and benefit from the skills presented in this book.

By making learning about fractions enjoyable, we hope to reveal a wonderful secret to your students—math is lots of fun!

NAME_____ DATE_____

Riddle 1

What should you do when two snails start fighting?

What To Do

Fill in the blanks with the correct answer. Match each answer to a letter in the Key. Then write the letter in the space above its problem number to find the answer to the riddle.

1 This pizza is divided into _____ equal slices.

2 This pizza is divided into _____ equal slices.

3 This pizza is divided into _____ equal slices.

4 This pizza is divided into _____ equal slices.

5 This pizza is divided into _____ equal slices.

6 This pizza is divided into _____ equal slices.

7 This pizza is divided into _____ equal slices.

8 This pizza is divided into _____ equal slices.

9 This pizza is divided into _____ equal slices.

10 This pizza is divided into _____ equal slices.

Key

20 . . . . A	4 . . . . O	11 X
3 . . . . T	50 . . . . F	9 . . . . T
8 . . . . U	7 . . . . G	18 . . . . B
10 . . . . U	16 . . . . E	2 . . . . M
6 . . . . S	12 I	5 L

Riddle Answer Let the ___ ___ ___ ___ ___ ___ ___ ___ ___ ___ ___ ___ .

2   **4 8 7 9**   **5 6**   **1 3 10**

NAME_____   DATE _____

Riddle 2

What did the egg do when it heard a joke?

Ha, Ha, Ha

What To Do

Answer the questions below. Match each answer to a letter in the Key. Then write the letter in the space above its problem number to find the answer to the riddle.

1 What fraction of the shapes are circles? _____

2 What fraction of the shapes are triangles? _____

3 What fraction of the shapes are shaded? _____

4 What fraction of the shapes have only three sides? _____

5 What fraction of the shapes are circles and squares? _____

6 What fraction of the shapes are not squares? _____

7 What fraction of the shapes are shaded? _____

8 What fraction of the shapes have no straight sides? _____

Key

1/8	O
4/7	C
3/8	D
6/7	W
6/9	K
1/9	R
3/7	E
7/9	S
2/5	E
3/4	C
2/3	A
1/2	D
5/8	R
1/5	M
3/5	T
5/6	A

Riddle Answer

I ___ ___ ___ ___ ___ ___ ___ ___ up!

3 **7** **5** **6** **2** **8** **4** **1**

NAME _____ DATE _____

Riddle 3

What do you get from an angry shark?

What To Do

Write the fractions that correspond to the words below.
Match each fraction to a letter in the Key. Then write the letter in the space above its problem number to find the answer to the riddle.

1 One-half = _____

2 One-third = _____

3 One-quarter = _____

4 One-sixth = _____

5 One-eighth = _____

6 One-seventh = _____

7 Two-thirds = _____

8 Three-quarters = _____

9 Three-fifths = _____

10 Two-sevenths = _____

Key

1/5 . . . . W	1/6 . . . . A	1/9 . . . . U
1/4 . . . . Y	2/3 . . . . A	1/8 . . . . S
3/5 . . . . W	1/7 . . . . A	4/5 . . . . K
1/2 . . . . F	2/2 . . . . M	3/4 . . . . A
2/7 . . . . R	1/3 . . . . A	1/25 . . . . E

Riddle Answer

___ ___   ___ ___ ___   ___ ___ ___ ___   ___ s possible
7 **5**   **1** **4** **10**   **6** **9** **2** **3**   **8**

NAME_____ DATE_____

Riddle 4

Which dance did the chicken refuse to do?

What To Do

Write the fractions that correspond to the words below.
Match each fraction to a letter in the Key. Then write the letter in the
space above its problem number to find the answer to the riddle.

1 Five-sixths = _____

2 Seven-elevenths = _____

3 Nine-sixteenths = _____

4 Five-eighths = _____

5 Seven-ninths = _____

6 Five-fourteenths = _____

7 Five-twelfths = _____

8 Twelve-thirteenths = _____

9 Eight-nineteenths = _____

10 Six-fifteenths = _____

Key

$7/13$ .... P	$7/11$ .... R	$5/6$ .... E
$5/13$ .... K	$8/19$ .... F	$6/15$ .... O
$5/8$ .... T	$5/7$ L	$7/8$ .... A
$9/16$ .... H	$5/14$ .... T	$5/12$ X
$1/4$ C	$12/13$ .... O	$7/9$ .... T

Riddle Answer

___ ___ ___   ___ ___ ___ - ___ ___ ___ ___
6 **3** **1**   **9** **10** **7**   **5** **2** **8** **4**

NAME_____ DATE _____

Riddle 5

Why did the monster need a third sock?

What To Do

Answer the questions below. Match each answer to a letter in the Key. Then write the letter in the space above its problem number to find the answer to the riddle.

1 In the fraction $\frac{5}{8}$, what is the **numerator**? _____

2 In the fraction $\frac{1}{7}$, what is the **denominator**? _____

3 In the fraction $\frac{3}{4}$, what is the **numerator**? _____

4 In the fraction $\frac{9}{10}$, what is the **denominator**? _____

5 Which is the **proper fraction**? $2\frac{1}{2}$ $\frac{3}{2}$ $\frac{1}{2}$

6 Which is the **improper fraction**? $2\frac{1}{2}$ $\frac{3}{2}$ $\frac{1}{2}$

7 Which is the **mixed number**? $2\frac{1}{2}$ $\frac{3}{2}$ $\frac{1}{2}$

8 Which is the **proper fraction**? $\frac{7}{6}$ $3\frac{1}{6}$ $\frac{5}{6}$

9 Which is the **improper fraction**? $\frac{7}{6}$ $3\frac{1}{6}$ $\frac{5}{6}$

10 Which is the **mixed number**? $\frac{7}{6}$ $3\frac{1}{6}$ $\frac{5}{6}$

Key

$\frac{1}{2}$	T
8	L
7	O
1	K
3	O
$\frac{7}{6}$	F
$\frac{5}{6}$	O
4	G
5	H
2	Z
$2\frac{1}{2}$	E
$3\frac{1}{6}$	N
10	T
$\frac{3}{2}$	R
9	A

Riddle Answer

He grew a __ __ __ __ __ __   __ __ __ __.
　　　　⑩ ❽ ❺ ❶ ❼ ❻ 　❾ ❷ ❸ ❹

NAME _____   DATE _____

Riddle 6

Why was six scared of seven?

What To Do

In each problem, circle the fraction that is NOT equivalent to the other fractions. Match each answer to a letter in the Key. Then write the letter in the space above its problem number to find the answer to the riddle.

1 $\dfrac{1}{2}$ $\dfrac{3}{4}$ $\dfrac{2}{4}$ **6** $\dfrac{20}{50}$ $\dfrac{2}{5}$ $\dfrac{5}{2}$

2 $\dfrac{2}{3}$ $\dfrac{6}{9}$ $\dfrac{3}{6}$ **7** $\dfrac{6}{7}$ $\dfrac{8}{10}$ $\dfrac{24}{30}$

3 $\dfrac{3}{8}$ $\dfrac{1}{4}$ $\dfrac{9}{24}$ **8** $\dfrac{1}{5}$ $\dfrac{7}{35}$ $\dfrac{6}{25}$

4 $\dfrac{4}{5}$ $\dfrac{6}{10}$ $\dfrac{3}{5}$ **9** $\dfrac{5}{15}$ $\dfrac{2}{3}$ $\dfrac{1}{3}$

5 $\dfrac{1}{9}$ $\dfrac{5}{45}$ $\dfrac{4}{10}$ **10** $\dfrac{1}{6}$ $\dfrac{3}{5}$ $\dfrac{15}{25}$

Key

$1/2$ .... B	$3/6$ I	$5/2$ .... E
$6/7$ V	$6/25$ .... A	$7/35$ .... R
$4/5$ .... N	$1/9$ V	$3/4$ .... E
$4/10$ .... N	$1/6$ .... N	$1/4$ .... T
$5/45$ .... O	$2/3$ .... E	$3/5$ .... S

Riddle Answer

Because se ___ ___ ___   " ___ ___ ___ "   ___ ___ ___ ___ .

NAME_____ DATE _____

Riddle 7

Who won the race between the two balls of string?

What To Do

Write the fractions below in simplest terms. Match each answer to a letter in the Key. Then write the letter in the space above its problem number to find the answer to the riddle.

1 $\frac{2}{4}$ = _____   **6** $\frac{6}{9}$ = _____

2 $\frac{3}{12}$ = _____   **7** $\frac{4}{10}$ = _____

3 $\frac{5}{15}$ = _____   **8** $\frac{12}{32}$ = _____

4 $\frac{4}{20}$ = _____   **9** $\frac{16}{36}$ = _____

5 $\frac{6}{8}$ = _____   **10** $\frac{10}{35}$ = _____

Key

3/8 .... D	1/6 L	1/3 .... W
2/3 .... R	4/9 .... E	1/4 .... E
1/2 .... E	3/5 .... P	3/4 .... E
4/7 .... O	2/5 I	5/6 .... K
2/7 .... T	1/8 .... A	1/5 .... Y

Riddle Answer

Th __ __ __ __ __ __ __ __ __ __ __ __.
    9 **4**   **3** **5** **6** **1**   **10** **7** **2** **8**

NAME_____ DATE _____

Riddle 8

What kind of dog did the vampire own?

What To Do

Write the fractions below in simplest terms. Match each answer to a letter in the Key. Then write the letter in the space above its problem number to find the answer to the riddle.

1 $\dfrac{25}{50}$ = _____

2 $\dfrac{32}{40}$ = _____

3 $\dfrac{24}{66}$ = _____

4 $\dfrac{45}{75}$ = _____

5 $\dfrac{26}{64}$ = _____

6 $\dfrac{10}{25}$ = _____

7 $\dfrac{27}{57}$ = _____

8 $\dfrac{48}{92}$ = _____

9 $\dfrac{35}{49}$ = _____

10 $\dfrac{60}{87}$ = _____

Key

12/23 .... D	9/19 .... O	1/5 C
3/5 .... N	4/11 L	5/7 .... O
2/5 .... H	10/23 I	9/22 .... A
3/8 .... M	20/29 .... O	13/32 .... B
12/27 .... A	4/5 .... U	1/2 .... D

Riddle Answer

A __ __ __ __ __ __ __ __ __ __
  5 **3** **10** **7** **1** **6** **9** **2** **4** **8**

NAME_____ DATE_____

Riddle 9 If I have 5 apples in one hand and 6 apples in the other, what would I have?

What To Do

Circle the correct answers below. Match each answer to a letter in the Key. Then write the letter in the space above its problem number to find the answer to the riddle.

Which fraction is greatest?

1 $\frac{1}{3}$ $\frac{1}{4}$ $\frac{1}{5}$

2 $\frac{2}{7}$ $\frac{5}{6}$ $\frac{6}{8}$

3 $\frac{4}{14}$ $\frac{8}{9}$ $\frac{12}{13}$

4 $\frac{7}{8}$ $\frac{9}{10}$ $\frac{6}{7}$

5 $\frac{15}{20}$ $\frac{12}{24}$ $\frac{18}{22}$

Which fraction is the least?

6 $\frac{4}{7}$ $\frac{2}{7}$ $\frac{5}{7}$

7 $\frac{3}{4}$ $\frac{2}{3}$ $\frac{1}{2}$

8 $\frac{7}{17}$ $\frac{4}{15}$ $\frac{6}{19}$

9 $\frac{16}{40}$ $\frac{25}{70}$ $\frac{42}{80}$

10 $\frac{24}{40}$ $\frac{12}{16}$ $\frac{18}{27}$

Key

12/13 . . . . A	5/6 . . . . B	2/3 . . . . U
3/4 . . . . F	24/40 . . . . N	6/8 . . . . E
9/10 . . . . H	25/70 . . . . G	18/22 . . . . S
1/3 . . . . W	4/15 . . . . D	4/14 . . . . T
1/2 . . . . O	1/5 . . . . K	2/7 I

Riddle Answer

T __ __   __ __ __   __ __ __ __ __
  1 **7**   **2** **6** **9**   **4** **3** **10** **8** **5**

NAME_____ DATE_____

Riddle 10

Why is it hard to play sports against a team of big cats?

What To Do

Rewrite the improper fractions below as mixed numbers. Write your answers in simplest terms. Match each answer to a letter in the Key. Then write the letter in the space above its problem number to find the answer to the riddle.

1 $\frac{6}{4}$ = _____

2 $\frac{10}{6}$ = _____

3 $\frac{13}{8}$ = _____

4 $\frac{21}{9}$ = _____

5 $\frac{15}{7}$ = _____

6 $\frac{36}{5}$ = _____

7 $\frac{23}{6}$ = _____

8 $\frac{16}{10}$ = _____

9 $\frac{47}{11}$ = _____

10 $\frac{16}{12}$ = _____

Key

$2\frac{1}{7}$ .... E	$2\frac{4}{9}$ .... O	$3\frac{1}{6}$ .... P
$2\frac{1}{3}$ C	$1\frac{2}{3}$ .... E	$4\frac{3}{11}$ .... T
$3\frac{8}{9}$ I	$1\frac{1}{2}$ .... B	$7\frac{1}{5}$ .... E
$3\frac{5}{6}$ .... A	$1\frac{5}{8}$ .... S	$2\frac{5}{7}$ .... R
$1\frac{1}{3}$ .... H	$4\frac{7}{11}$ .... M	$1\frac{3}{5}$ .... H

Riddle Answer

They might __ __ ___ __ __ __ __ __ __ __ __.

NAME_____ DATE _____

Riddle 11

Why did the hen run away?

What To Do

Rewrite the mixed numbers below as improper fractions.
Match each answer to a letter in the Key. Then write the letter in the space
above its problem number to find the answer to the riddle.

❶ $3\frac{2}{5}$ = _____   ❻ $6\frac{2}{3}$ = _____

❷ $7\frac{3}{4}$ = _____   ❼ $9\frac{1}{2}$ = _____

❸ $2\frac{1}{3}$ = _____   ❽ $8\frac{3}{4}$ = _____

❹ $1\frac{1}{2}$ = _____   ❾ $7\frac{5}{6}$ = _____

❺ $4\frac{3}{5}$ = _____   ❿ $5\frac{1}{4}$ = _____

Key

$18/3$ . . . . O	$17/5$ C	$23/5$ C
$7/3$ . . . . K	$35/4$ I	$33/4$ . . . . U
$7/6$ . . . . M	$18/7$ . . . . J	$19/2$ . . . . E
$21/4$ . . . . S	$3/2$ . . . . A	$47/6$ . . . . H
$20/3$ . . . . W	$31/4$ . . . . N	$50/4$ V

Riddle Answer

She ⎯ ⎯ ⎯   ⎯ ⎯ ⎯ ⎯ ⎯ ⎯ ⎯ ⎯.
    ❻ ❹ ❿ ❺ ❾ ❽ ❶ ❸ ❼ ❷

NAME_____ DATE_____

Riddle 12

What does a lion lawyer study?

What To Do

Solve the addition problems below. Write your answers in simplest terms. Match each answer to a letter in the Key. Then write the letter in the space above its problem number to find the answer to the riddle.

1 $\frac{1}{2} + \frac{1}{2}$ = _____

2 $\frac{1}{4} + \frac{1}{4}$ = _____

3 $\frac{1}{6} + \frac{3}{6}$ = _____

4 $\frac{1}{5} + \frac{3}{5}$ = _____

5 $\frac{4}{7} + \frac{2}{7}$ = _____

6 $\frac{3}{8} + \frac{2}{8}$ = _____

7 $\frac{5}{9} + \frac{2}{9}$ = _____

8 $\frac{2}{6} + \frac{3}{6}$ = _____

9 $\frac{1}{8} + \frac{5}{8}$ = _____

10 $\frac{3}{9} + \frac{1}{9}$ = _____

Key

$5/6$ . . . . J	$6/7$ L	$3/4$ . . . . E
$7/8$ . . . . A	2 I	$7/9$ . . . . G
$4/9$ . . . . H	$4/5$ . . . . E	$2/5$ . . . . M
$1/2$ . . . . T	1 . . . . U	$5/8$ . . . . F
$2/3$ . . . . N	$3/8$ . . . . B	$2/7$ . . . . O

Riddle Answer

The law o ___  ___ ___ ___  ___ ___ ___ ___ ___

6 **2** **10** **4**   **8** **1** **3** **7** **5** **9**

NAME _____ DATE _____

Riddle 13

Where do ghosts go swimming?

What To Do

Solve the addition problems below. Write your answers in simplest terms. Match each answer to a letter in the Key. Then write the letter in the space above its problem number to find the answer to the riddle.

1 $\dfrac{2}{3} + \dfrac{2}{3} =$ _____

2 $\dfrac{3}{4} + \dfrac{2}{4} =$ _____

3 $\dfrac{3}{5} + \dfrac{4}{5} =$ _____

4 $\dfrac{4}{6} + \dfrac{5}{6} =$ _____

5 $\dfrac{7}{9} + \dfrac{6}{9} =$ _____

6 $\dfrac{4}{8} + \dfrac{7}{8} =$ _____

7 $\dfrac{5}{11} + \dfrac{7}{11} =$ _____

8 $\dfrac{8}{9} + \dfrac{8}{9} =$ _____

9 $\dfrac{12}{15} + \dfrac{10}{15} =$ _____

10 $\dfrac{8}{12} + \dfrac{6}{12} =$ _____

Key

$1\ ^7/_{15}$ . . . . A	$1\ ^1/_{11}$ . . . . D	$1\ ^1/_3$ . . . . D
$1\ ^3/_8$ . . . . S	$1\ ^1/_4$ . . . . E	$1\ ^5/_8$ I
$1\ ^2/_5$ . . . . A	$1\ ^1/_6$ . . . . E	$1\ ^4/_5$ . . . . M
$1\ ^2/_3$ . . . . O	$1\ ^3/_4$ . . . . G	$1\ ^4/_9$ . . . . E
$1\ ^5/_6$ . . . . N	$1\ ^1/_2$ . . . . H	$1\ ^7/_9$ . . . . T

Riddle Answer

___ ___ ___   ___ ___ ___ ___   ___ ___ ___
8 **4** **10** **7** **2** **9** **1** **6** **5** **3**

NAME_____ DATE_____

Riddle 14

How do you stop a rhinoceros from charging?

What To Do

Solve the addition problems below. Write your answers in simplest terms. Match each answer to a letter in the Key. Then write the letter in the space above its problem number to find the answer to the riddle.

1 $\dfrac{11}{15} + \dfrac{13}{15} =$ _____

2 $\dfrac{17}{24} + \dfrac{20}{24} =$ _____

3 $\dfrac{28}{35} + \dfrac{20}{35} =$ _____

4 $\dfrac{22}{27} + \dfrac{9}{27} =$ _____

5 $\dfrac{7}{36} + \dfrac{31}{36} =$ _____

6 $\dfrac{23}{40} + \dfrac{17}{40} =$ _____

7 $\dfrac{18}{19} + \dfrac{8}{19} =$ _____

8 $\dfrac{32}{45} + \dfrac{42}{45} =$ _____

9 $\dfrac{27}{52} + \dfrac{38}{52} =$ _____

10 $\dfrac{26}{63} + \dfrac{40}{63} =$ _____

Key

$1\,^2/_3$ L	$1\,^4/_{27}$ .... E	$1\,^3/_5$ .... R
$1\,^{13}/_{24}$ I	$1\,^6/_{39}$ .... O	$1\,^7/_{19}$ .... D
$1\,^5/_8$ .... K	$1\,^{17}/_{23}$ .... W	1 .... R
$1\,^1/_{18}$ .... D	$1\,^{29}/_{45}$ .... S	$1\,^{13}/_{35}$ C
$1\,^1/_4$ .... T	$1\,^1/_2$ .... M	$1\,^1/_{21}$ .... A

Riddle Answer

Take away its c __ __ __ __ __ __ __ __ __ __ .

6 **4** **7** **2** **9** **3** **10** **1** **5** **8**

NAME _____ DATE _____

Riddle 15

Why didn't the dog want to play ball?

What To Do

Solve the subtraction problems below. Write your answers in simplest terms. Match each answer to a letter in the Key. Then write the letter in the space above its problem number to find the answer to the riddle.

1 $\frac{3}{4} - \frac{2}{4} =$ _____

2 $\frac{7}{8} - \frac{4}{8} =$ _____

3 $\frac{3}{5} - \frac{1}{5} =$ _____

4 $\frac{5}{6} - \frac{3}{6} =$ _____

5 $\frac{4}{5} - \frac{3}{5} =$ _____

6 $\frac{4}{7} - \frac{1}{7} =$ _____

7 $\frac{3}{9} - \frac{2}{9} =$ _____

8 $\frac{6}{8} - \frac{5}{8} =$ _____

9 $\frac{5}{7} - \frac{3}{7} =$ _____

10 $\frac{3}{6} - \frac{2}{6} =$ _____

Key

$3/7$ .... O	$1/2$ .... W	$2/5$ .... A
$4/7$ I	$3/5$ .... D	$7/8$ C
$1/5$ .... B	$3/8$ .... T	$1/3$ .... R
$1/8$ X	$1/9$ .... W	$2/9$ .... U
$1/4$ .... S	$2/7$ .... E	$1/6$ .... A

Riddle Answer

I  __ __ __ __  __ __ __ __ __ .
   2   **7** **3** **1**   **10**   **5** **6** **8** **9** **4**

NAME _____ DATE _____

Riddle 16

Where did the monster go when she lost her hand?

What To Do

Solve the subtraction problems below. Write your answers in simplest terms. Match each answer to a letter in the Key. Then write the letter in the space above its problem number to find the answer to the riddle.

1 $\dfrac{8}{9} - \dfrac{2}{9} =$ _____

2 $\dfrac{13}{15} - \dfrac{4}{15} =$ _____

3 $\dfrac{18}{20} - \dfrac{9}{20} =$ _____

4 $\dfrac{20}{32} - \dfrac{8}{32} =$ _____

5 $\dfrac{23}{25} - \dfrac{20}{25} =$ _____

6 $\dfrac{30}{34} - \dfrac{16}{34} =$ _____

7 $\dfrac{21}{40} - \dfrac{5}{40} =$ _____

8 $\dfrac{38}{52} - \dfrac{10}{52} =$ _____

9 $\dfrac{12}{18} - \dfrac{9}{18} =$ _____

10 $\dfrac{40}{45} - \dfrac{20}{45} =$ _____

Key

$2/5$ .... N	$4/9$ .... O	$9/20$ .... P
$8/17$ .... R	$3/8$ .... A	$2/9$ I
$1/6$ .... D	$3/25$ .... S	$7/13$ .... H
$2/3$ .... N	$7/17$ .... H	$1/3$ V
$1/2$ .... K	$1/5$ .... Q	$3/5$ .... D

Riddle Answer

A seco ___ ___ - ___ ___ ___ ___   ___ ___ ___ ___
7 **2**   **6** **4** **1** **9**   **5** **8** **10** **3**

NAME_____ DATE_____

Riddle 17

What is big, gray, and flies straight up?

What To Do

Solve the addition problems below. Write your answers in simplest terms. Match each answer to a letter in the Key. Then write the letter in the space above its problem number to find the answer to the riddle.

1 $1\frac{1}{2}$ + $1\frac{1}{2}$ = _____

2 $2\frac{1}{4}$ + $1\frac{3}{4}$ = _____

3 $5\frac{1}{3}$ + $3\frac{1}{3}$ = _____

4 $4\frac{1}{6}$ + $2\frac{3}{6}$ = _____

5 $1\frac{2}{5}$ + $6\frac{2}{5}$ = _____

6 $3\frac{3}{7}$ + $6\frac{5}{7}$ = _____

7 $8\frac{4}{9}$ + $5\frac{8}{9}$ = _____

8 $4\frac{3}{8}$ + $6\frac{6}{8}$ = _____

9 $3\frac{7}{9}$ + $1\frac{6}{9}$ = _____

10 $2\frac{2}{8}$ + $3\frac{7}{8}$ = _____

Key

$11\frac{1}{8}$ L	4 .... T	$8\frac{2}{3}$ .... P
$6\frac{2}{3}$ .... E	$14\frac{1}{3}$ .... N	$6\frac{1}{8}$ .... E
2 .... U	3 .... O	12 .... D
16 .... M	$10\frac{1}{7}$ C	$7\frac{4}{5}$ .... R
$5\frac{4}{9}$ .... E	15 .... K	1 C

Riddle Answer

A __ ' __ __ __ __ __ __ __ __ __

  7   **4** **8** **10** **6** **1** **3** **2** **9** **5**

NAME_____ DATE _____

Riddle 18

Why did the tennis player hit the ball softly?

What To Do

Solve the subtraction problems below. Write your answers in simplest terms. Match each answer to a letter in the Key. Then write the letter in the space above its problem number to find the answer to the riddle.

❶ $2\frac{2}{3} - 1\frac{1}{3} =$ _____

❷ $5\frac{4}{5} - 3\frac{2}{5} =$ _____

❸ $8\frac{5}{7} - 6\frac{3}{7} =$ _____

❹ $4\frac{3}{4} - 1\frac{1}{4} =$ _____

❺ $6\frac{3}{8} - 4\frac{1}{8} =$ _____

❻ $9\frac{4}{5} - 5\frac{1}{5} =$ _____

❼ $7\frac{7}{9} - 3\frac{4}{9} =$ _____

❽ $10\frac{5}{6} - 7\frac{4}{6} =$ _____

❾ $3\frac{4}{5} - 2\frac{3}{5} =$ _____

❿ $5\frac{6}{7} - 3\frac{2}{7} =$ _____

Key

$3\frac{1}{6}$ .... A	$2\frac{1}{4}$ C	$1\frac{2}{3}$ .... S
$4\frac{5}{8}$ .... U	$3\frac{2}{5}$ .... P	$4\frac{3}{5}$ .... T
$3\frac{1}{2}$ .... A	$1\frac{1}{3}$ .... K	$2\frac{2}{5}$ .... R
$1\frac{1}{5}$ .... E	$4\frac{1}{3}$ .... K	$2\frac{2}{6}$ .... M
$2\frac{5}{7}$ .... B	$2\frac{2}{7}$ .... M	$2\frac{4}{7}$ .... E

Riddle Answer

So he wouldn't  __ __ __ __   a __ __ __ __ __ __ .
      ❸ ❹ ❼ ❾   ❷ ❽ ❺ ❶ ❿ ❻

NAME_____ DATE_____

Riddle 19

Why couldn't the ghost tell a lie?

What To Do

Solve the addition problems below. Write your answers in simplest terms. Match each answer to a letter in the Key. Then write the letter in the space above its problem number to find the answer to the riddle.

1 $\dfrac{1}{2} + \dfrac{1}{3} =$ _____

2 $\dfrac{2}{5} + \dfrac{1}{4} =$ _____

3 $\dfrac{1}{6} + \dfrac{4}{9} =$ _____

4 $\dfrac{3}{10} + \dfrac{2}{5} =$ _____

5 $\dfrac{2}{7} + \dfrac{1}{5} =$ _____

6 $\dfrac{1}{3} + \dfrac{1}{4} =$ _____

7 $\dfrac{2}{3} + \dfrac{2}{6} =$ _____

8 $\dfrac{2}{9} + \dfrac{1}{3} =$ _____

9 $\dfrac{2}{14} + \dfrac{1}{2} =$ _____

10 $\dfrac{3}{8} + \dfrac{1}{4} =$ _____

Key

$5/9$ .... H	$9/14$ .... O	$17/35$ I
$3/10$ .... E	$11/18$ .... H	$5/6$ .... H
2 .... A	$4/9$ .... K	$3/4$ .... S
$5/8$ .... R	1 .... G	$13/20$ .... M
6 .... J	$7/10$ .... U	$7/12$ .... T

Riddle Answer

You can see right __ __ __ __ __ __ __ __ __ __ __.

6 **3** **10** **9** **4** **7** **8** **1** **5** **2**

NAME_____ DATE _____

Riddle 20

What do you get if you cross a sheepdog with a tulip?

What To Do

Solve the addition problems below. Write your answers in simplest terms. Match each answer to a letter in the Key. Then write the letter in the space above its problem number to find the answer to the riddle.

1 $\dfrac{3}{4} + \dfrac{1}{2} =$ _____

2 $\dfrac{5}{6} + \dfrac{5}{8} =$ _____

3 $\dfrac{2}{7} + \dfrac{3}{5} =$ _____

4 $\dfrac{3}{8} + \dfrac{4}{5} =$ _____

5 $\dfrac{7}{9} + \dfrac{4}{6} =$ _____

6 $\dfrac{10}{11} + \dfrac{1}{4} =$ _____

7 $\dfrac{4}{15} + \dfrac{7}{10} =$ _____

8 $\dfrac{9}{20} + \dfrac{3}{18} =$ _____

9 $\dfrac{14}{15} + \dfrac{11}{30} =$ _____

10 $\dfrac{13}{25} + \dfrac{11}{20} =$ _____

Key

$41/50$ .... B	$1\ 3/10$ L	$31/35$ .... E
$29/30$ .... O	$1\ 4/9$ I	$1\ 7/40$ L
$2\ 4/5$ .... A	$1\ 17/55$ .... U	$1\ 7/100$ .... W
$1\ 11/24$ ...... F	$1\ 7/44$ L	$37/60$ .... R
$31/47$ X	$1\ 7/11$ .... M	$1\ 1/4$ .... E

Riddle Answer

A co __ __ __ __ - __ __ __ __ __ __
    9 **4** **5** **1**   **2** **6** **7** **10** **3** **8**

NAME_____ DATE_____

Riddle 21

What did the orangutan call his wife?

What To Do

Solve the subtraction problems below. Write your answers in simplest terms. Match each answer to a letter in the Key. Then write the letter in the space above its problem number to find the answer to the riddle.

1 $\frac{7}{10} - \frac{2}{5} =$ _____

2 $\frac{3}{4} - \frac{1}{2} =$ _____

3 $\frac{5}{6} - \frac{1}{3} =$ _____

4 $\frac{13}{15} - \frac{2}{3} =$ _____

5 $\frac{9}{12} - \frac{3}{4} =$ _____

6 $\frac{10}{24} - \frac{3}{8} =$ _____

7 $\frac{28}{36} - \frac{4}{6} =$ _____

8 $\frac{7}{16} - \frac{1}{4} =$ _____

9 $\frac{48}{50} - \frac{20}{25} =$ _____

10 $\frac{20}{42} - \frac{3}{7} =$ _____

1/24 .... A	1/5 .... E	1/9 .... P
1/8 .... W	4/25 .... T	3/5 .... S
1/21 .... S	1/25 .... O	5/16 .... K
1/2 .... E	3/10 .... M	0 .... R
1/4 .... M	3/16 I	1/15 .... N

Riddle Answer

Hi __ __ __ __ __ __ - __ __ __ __
   10 **7** **5** **8** **1** **3** **2** **6** **9** **4**

NAME_____ DATE _____

Riddle 22

What do you say when you meet a two-headed dragon?

What To Do

Solve the subtraction problems below. Write your answers in simplest terms. Match each answer to a letter in the Key. Then write the letter in the space above its problem number to find the answer to the riddle.

1 $\frac{4}{7} - \frac{1}{3} =$ _____

2 $\frac{5}{8} - \frac{1}{2} =$ _____

3 $\frac{7}{11} - \frac{1}{4} =$ _____

4 $\frac{7}{8} - \frac{2}{3} =$ _____

5 $\frac{9}{10} - \frac{2}{6} =$ _____

6 $\frac{7}{15} - \frac{3}{8} =$ _____

7 $\frac{5}{9} - \frac{1}{2} =$ _____

8 $\frac{4}{15} - \frac{1}{6} =$ _____

9 $\frac{9}{20} - \frac{2}{8} =$ _____

10 $\frac{20}{32} - \frac{2}{6} =$ _____

Key

$13/120$ .... U	$1/10$ .... E	$17/44$ L
$5/21$ .... E	$23/44$ .... A	$3/8$ .... R
$1/8$ L	$11/120$ L	$1/18$ .... H
$7/24$ .... O	$10/21$ .... M	$1/5$ .... O
$3/5$ .... P	$5/24$ L	$17/30$ .... H

Riddle Answer

"___ ___ ___ ___ ___! ___ ___ ___ ___ ___ ___!"
5 **8** **3** **6** **10**   **7** **1** **4** **2** **9**

NAME _____ DATE _____

Riddle 23

What did one keyboard say to another keyboard?

What To Do

Solve the addition and subtraction problems below. Write your answers in simplest terms. Match each answer to a letter in the Key. Then write the letter in the space above its problem number to find the answer to the riddle.

1 $\dfrac{5}{8} - \dfrac{9}{20} =$ _____

2 $\dfrac{3}{4} + \dfrac{1}{11} =$ _____

3 $\dfrac{1}{2} - \dfrac{5}{13} =$ _____

4 $\dfrac{2}{3} + \dfrac{2}{9} =$ _____

5 $\dfrac{5}{6} - \dfrac{7}{15} =$ _____

6 $\dfrac{7}{10} + \dfrac{9}{30} =$ _____

7 $\dfrac{8}{12} - \dfrac{3}{32} =$ _____

8 $\dfrac{3}{8} + \dfrac{4}{10} =$ _____

9 $\dfrac{4}{5} - \dfrac{8}{20} =$ _____

10 $\dfrac{5}{12} + \dfrac{20}{36} =$ _____

Key

$4/5$ . . . . W	$13/26$ . . . . B	$9/44$ . . . . D
$7/18$ . . . . U	$7/40$ . . . . M	$8/9$ . . . . Y
$11/30$ . . . . Y	$55/96$ . . . . T	$3/26$ . . . . E
1 . . . . U	$2/5$ . . . . E	$37/44$ . . . . A
$35/36$ . . . . P	$1/2$ C	$31/40$ . . . . R

Riddle Answer

"Yo ___ ___ ___ ___ ___ ___ ___ ___ ___ ___."
  6   **2** **8** **9**   **1** **5**   **7** **4** **10** **3**

NAME _____ DATE _____

Riddle 24

What do frogs say when they meet each other?

What To Do

Solve the addition problems below. Write your answers in simplest terms. Match each answer to a letter in the Key. Then write the letter in the space above its problem number to find the answer to the riddle.

1 $2\frac{1}{2} + 4\frac{1}{4} =$ _____

2 $4\frac{1}{5} + 3\frac{3}{10} =$ _____

3 $6\frac{2}{3} + 5\frac{1}{6} =$ _____

4 $1\frac{1}{8} + 3\frac{3}{4} =$ _____

5 $7\frac{2}{9} + 4\frac{5}{12} =$ _____

6 $8\frac{3}{5} + 2\frac{7}{15} =$ _____

7 $3\frac{3}{7} + 4\frac{6}{21} =$ _____

8 $5\frac{2}{6} + 1\frac{4}{30} =$ _____

9 $10\frac{1}{2} + 6\frac{1}{8} =$ _____

10 $9\frac{5}{6} + 3\frac{1}{9} =$ _____

Key

$12\,^{13}/_{18}$ ..... A	$6\,^{3}/_{4}$ .... U	$7\,^{1}/_{2}$ .... T
$7\,^{5}/_{7}$ .... Y	$4\,^{5}/_{8}$ .... P	$6\,^{2}/_{3}$ .... M
$4\,^{7}/_{8}$ .... W	$11\,^{5}/_{6}$ .... H	$16\,^{5}/_{8}$ I
$6\,^{7}/_{15}$ ...... N	$11\,^{1}/_{15}$ ...... W	$11\,^{1}/_{6}$ .... J
$10\,^{27}/_{50}$ I	$12\,^{17}/_{18}$ ..... E	$11\,^{23}/_{36}$ ..... O

Riddle Answer

"Warts ___ ___ ___ ___ ___ ___ ___ ___ ___ ___**?"**
   8 10 6   4 9 2 3   7 5 1

NAME _____ DATE _____

Riddle 25

What kind of horse always looks fashionable?

What To Do

Solve the subtraction problems below. Write your answers in simplest terms. Match each answer to a letter in the Key. Then write the letter in the space above its problem number to find the answer to the riddle.

1 $6\frac{3}{4} - 4\frac{1}{2} =$ _____

2 $5\frac{3}{8} - 2\frac{1}{4} =$ _____

3 $9\frac{4}{6} - 7\frac{1}{3} =$ _____

4 $12\frac{1}{2} - 8\frac{3}{8} =$ _____

5 $10\frac{2}{3} - 5\frac{1}{4} =$ _____

6 $7\frac{3}{5} - 4\frac{1}{3} =$ _____

7 $15\frac{2}{5} - 9\frac{2}{7} =$ _____

8 $8\frac{5}{6} - 4\frac{4}{5} =$ _____

9 $14\frac{9}{11} - 3\frac{3}{4} =$ _____

10 $20\frac{8}{9} - 13\frac{2}{3} =$ _____

Key

$3\frac{3}{8}$ ....U	$6\frac{4}{35}$ ....H	$7\frac{2}{9}$ ....S
$4\frac{1}{8}$ ....E	$4\frac{1}{30}$ ....S	$6\frac{7}{35}$ ....D
$2\frac{1}{3}$ ....O	$2\frac{1}{2}$ ....A	$3\frac{4}{15}$ ....O
$2\frac{1}{4}$ ....T	$3\frac{1}{8}$ ....R	$2\frac{2}{3}$ ....M
$5\frac{7}{12}$ X	$11\frac{3}{44}$ ......H	$5\frac{5}{12}$ ....E

Riddle Answer

A cl __ __ __ __ __ __ __ __ __ __
   6 **1** **9** **5** **10** **7** **3** **2** **8** **4**

NAME_____ DATE_____

Riddle 26

What did the hot dog say to the hamburger?

What To Do

Write the decimal equivalents of the fractions below. Match each answer to a letter in the Key. Then write the letter in the space above its problem number to find the answer to the riddle.

1 $\frac{4}{5}$ = _____

2 $\frac{3}{4}$ = _____

3 $\frac{1}{2}$ = _____

4 $\frac{3}{5}$ = _____

5 $\frac{1}{4}$ = _____

6 $\frac{1}{8}$ = _____

7 $\frac{3}{8}$ = _____

8 $\frac{2}{5}$ = _____

9 $\frac{5}{8}$ = _____

10 $\frac{9}{10}$ = _____

Key

0.375 C	0.75 . . . . O	0.325 . . . . S
0.825 . . . . J	0.2 I	0.4 . . . . T
0.5 . . . . N	0.125 . . . . A	0.25 . . . . E
0.425 . . . . B	0.625 I	0.8 . . . . T
0.9 . . . . E	0.6 . . . . M	0.675 . . . . Y

Riddle Answer

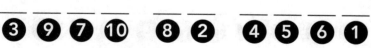

" ___ ___ ___ ___ ___ ___ ___ ___ ___ ___ you!"
  3 **9** **7** **10** **8** **2** **4** **5** **6** **1**

NAME_____ DATE_____

Riddle 27

If you had 10 cows and 10 goats, what would you have? What To Do

Write the decimal equivalents of the improper fractions below.
Match each answer to a letter in the Key. Then write the letter in the space
above its problem number to find the answer to the riddle.

1 $\frac{5}{2}$ = _____

2 $\frac{17}{4}$ = _____

3 $\frac{8}{5}$ = _____

4 $\frac{36}{5}$ = _____

5 $\frac{42}{8}$ = _____

6 $\frac{56}{5}$ = _____

7 $\frac{26}{8}$ = _____

8 $\frac{19}{2}$ = _____

9 $\frac{87}{15}$ = _____

10 $\frac{71}{10}$ = _____

Key

2.5 L	6.7 .... E	5.25 .... O
2.1 .... P	1.6 .... K	9.6 .... U
9.5 .... M	7.1 I	3.25 .... F
11.2 .... T	4.25 .... O	7.5 .... N
7.2 .... S	13.1 .... A	5.8 L

Riddle Answer

___ ___ ___ ___ ___ ___ ___ ___ ___ ___

9 **5** **6** **4** **2** **7** **8** **10** **1** **3**

NAME _____ DATE _____

Riddle 28

When is the best time to tell a joke?

What To Do

Circle the correct answers below. Match each answer to a letter in the Key. Then write the letter in the space above its problem number to find the answer to the riddle.

1 Which is the **greatest**?   0.05 $\frac{1}{2}$ 0.2

2 Which is the **greatest**? $\frac{2}{3}$ 0.75   0.6

3 Which is the **greatest**?   1.2 $\frac{6}{4}$ $2\frac{1}{2}$

4 Which is the **greatest**?   3.25 $\frac{9}{4}$ $3\frac{2}{3}$

5 Which is the **greatest**? $\frac{12}{5}$ 1.25 $4\frac{1}{2}$

6 Which is the **least**?   0.04   0.4 $\frac{1}{4}$

7 Which is the **least**? $\frac{32}{100}$ 3.2   0.032

8 Which is the **least**? $\frac{16}{8}$ 2.1 $2\frac{1}{5}$

9 Which is the **least**? $\frac{29}{6}$ 2.96 $4\frac{1}{3}$

10 Which is the **least**?   5.6 $5\frac{1}{6}$ $\frac{45}{7}$

Key

0.032	G
0.05	B
0.75	U
$2\frac{1}{2}$	T
$\frac{2}{3}$	O
$\frac{1}{2}$	N
2.96	R
$\frac{16}{8}$	O
$\frac{6}{4}$	C
$5\frac{1}{6}$	L
$3\frac{2}{3}$	E
$\frac{12}{5}$	L
$4\frac{1}{2}$	H
1.25	R
0.04	A

Riddle Answer

In the ___ ___ ___ ___ ___ ___ ___ ___ – ___ ___ **on**

⑩ ⑥ ② ⑦ ⑤ ③ ④ ⑨   ① ⑧

NAME_____ DATE_____

Riddle 29

What is a baby elephant after she is eight weeks old?

What To Do

Rewrite the ratios below as fractions. Write your answers in simplest terms. Match each answer to a letter in the Key. Then write the letter in the space above its problem number to find the answer to the riddle.

1   1:4   =   _____

2   11:16 =   _____

3   8:20 =   _____

4   15:25 =   _____

5   6:7   =   _____

6   14:33 =   _____

7   26:39 =   _____

8   2:23 =   _____

9   32:40 =   _____

10   40:55 =   _____

Key

4 . . . . Q	$2\frac{1}{2}$ . . . . M	$^2/_{23}$ L
$^8/_{11}$ . . . . E	$^4/_5$ . . . . D	$^{12}/_{20}$ . . . . P
$^6/_7$ . . . . E	$^1/_4$ . . . . K	$^{14}/_{43}$ . . . . A
$^2/_5$ . . . . N	$1\frac{5}{11}$ . . . . Z	$^2/_3$ . . . . E
$^{14}/_{33}$ . . . . . . W	$^{11}/_{16}$ . . . . S	$^3/_5$ . . . . O

Riddle Answer

Ni __ __   __ __ __ __ __ __   __ __ __

  3 **10**   **6** **5** **7** **1** **2**   **4** **8** **9**

NAME _____ DATE _____

Riddle 30

What is a frog's favorite shoe?

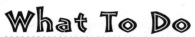

Solve the multiplication problems below. Write your answers in simplest terms. Match each answer to a letter in the Key. Then write the letter in the space above its problem number to find the answer to the riddle.

1 $\frac{1}{2} \times \frac{1}{3} =$ _____

2 $\frac{3}{4} \times \frac{1}{7} =$ _____

3 $\frac{2}{5} \times \frac{3}{8} =$ _____

4 $\frac{4}{7} \times \frac{2}{3} =$ _____

5 $\frac{1}{8} \times \frac{5}{6} =$ _____

6 $\frac{2}{9} \times \frac{1}{2} =$ _____

7 $\frac{2}{4} \times \frac{3}{7} =$ _____

8 $\frac{3}{4} \times \frac{2}{6} =$ _____

9 $\frac{6}{9} \times \frac{3}{5} =$ _____

10 $\frac{3}{8} \times \frac{5}{7} =$ _____

Key

$1/9$ .... T	$18/56$ .... F	$3/28$ .... A
$8/21$ .... A	$2/5$ .... D	$1/8$ .... H
$7/48$ .... E	$3/14$ .... N	$5/48$ .... A
$3/20$ .... D	$8/23$ .... G	$3/4$ I
$1/6$ .... O	$15/56$ .... S	$1/4$ L

Riddle Answer

An open- ___ ___ ___ ___   ___ ___ ___ ___ ___ ___

❻ ❶ ❹ ❾   ❿ ❷ ❼ ❸ ❺ ❽

NAME _____ DATE _____

Riddle 31

What did the elephant say when his tail was grabbed?

What To Do

Solve the multiplication problems below. Write your answers in simplest terms. Match each answer to a letter in the Key. Then write the letter in the space above its problem number to find the answer to the riddle.

1 $\frac{4}{9} \times \frac{3}{4} =$ _____

2 $\frac{5}{7} \times \frac{2}{3} =$ _____

3 $\frac{9}{10} \times \frac{6}{8} =$ _____

4 $\frac{8}{9} \times \frac{6}{7} =$ _____

5 $\frac{2}{5} \times \frac{4}{5} =$ _____

6 $\frac{7}{9} \times \frac{3}{8} =$ _____

7 $\frac{4}{7} \times \frac{9}{11} =$ _____

8 $\frac{7}{8} \times \frac{2}{9} =$ _____

9 $\frac{2}{3} \times \frac{5}{8} =$ _____

10 $\frac{3}{4} \times \frac{5}{6} =$ _____

Key

$16/21$ .... O	$2/3$ C	$7/24$ .... F
$5/12$ .... M	$5/8$ .... E	$10/21$ .... N
$34/77$ .... A	$8/25$ .... H	$3/8$ .... K
$1/3$ .... T	$36/77$ .... D	$9/24$ I
$27/40$ .... E	$7/12$ L	$7/36$ .... E

Riddle Answer

"That's _____ ___ ____   ___ ___ ___   ___ ___   ___ ___ !"
       1 **5** **10**   **8** **2** **7**   **4** **6**   **9** **3**

NAME_____   DATE_____

Riddle 32

How do squirrels feel when you hide their food?

What To Do

Solve the multiplication problems below. Write your answers in simplest terms. Match each answer to a letter in the Key. Then write the letter in the space above its problem number to find the answer to the riddle.

1 $\frac{1}{4} \times 4 =$ _____

2 $\frac{2}{3} \times 6 =$ _____

3 $\frac{3}{5} \times 3 =$ _____

4 $\frac{4}{6} \times 2 =$ _____

5 $\frac{5}{7} \times 1 =$ _____

6 $\frac{6}{8} \times 4 =$ _____

7 $\frac{7}{9} \times 5 =$ _____

8 $\frac{8}{10} \times 2 =$ _____

9 $\frac{9}{11} \times 3 =$ _____

10 $\frac{10}{12} \times 6 =$ _____

Key

3 . . . . T	$5/7$ . . . . H	5 . . . . E
$1\,1/3$ . . . . S	$1/2$ . . . . B	$3/4$ . . . . K
12 . . . . A	1 . . . . N	$2\,5/11$ . . . . M
$1\,4/5$ . . . . E	15 I	$2/3$ . . . . Y
4 . . . . S	$1\,3/5$ . . . . U	$3\,8/9$ . . . . T

Riddle Answer

It driv ___ ___ ___ ___ ___ ___ ___ ___ ___ ___!
⑩ ④ ⑦ ⑤ ③ ⑨ ① ⑧ ⑥ ②

NAME_____ DATE _____

Riddle 33

Why were the elephants asked to leave the swimming pool?

What To Do

Solve the multiplication problems below. Write your answers in simplest terms. Match each answer to a letter in the Key. Then write the letter in the space above its problem number to find the answer to the riddle.

1 $\frac{1}{3} \times \frac{15}{2} =$ _____

2 $\frac{1}{2} \times \frac{22}{4} =$ _____

3 $\frac{1}{3} \times \frac{81}{8} =$ _____

4 $\frac{1}{4} \times \frac{36}{5} =$ _____

5 $\frac{1}{5} \times \frac{95}{10} =$ _____

6 $\frac{2}{3} \times 8\frac{1}{4} =$ _____

7 $\frac{7}{8} \times 4\frac{4}{7} =$ _____

8 $\frac{6}{7} \times 2\frac{3}{9} =$ _____

9 $\frac{4}{5} \times 7\frac{3}{6} =$ _____

10 $\frac{8}{10} \times 5\frac{1}{4} =$ _____

Key

$1\,^9/_{10}$ .... R	4 .... K	$1\,^3/_4$ .... O
2 .... S	3 .... A	$2\,^1/_2$ .... P
$4\,^1/_5$ .... T	$3\,^3/_8$ .... E	$6\,^1/_3$ .... W
$4\,^1/_2$ .... M	$5\,^1/_2$ .... N	$2\,^3/_4$ .... U
$1\,^4/_5$ .... K	5 .... D	6 .... E

Riddle Answer

They couldn't __ __ __ __ **their** __ __ __ __ __ __ **up.**

NAME_____ **DATE**_____

Riddle 34

What do you call cows that can't produce milk?

What To Do

Solve the multiplication problems below. Write your answers in simplest terms. Match each answer to a letter in the Key. Then write the letter in the space above its problem number to find the answer to the riddle.

1 $1\frac{3}{5}$ x $2\frac{1}{2}$ = _____

2 $4\frac{1}{5}$ x $6\frac{2}{3}$ = _____

3 $8\frac{1}{4}$ x $2\frac{2}{9}$ = _____

4 $5\frac{5}{6}$ x $6\frac{3}{5}$ = _____

5 $2\frac{6}{8}$ x $8\frac{2}{11}$ = _____

6 $3\frac{2}{3}$ x $5\frac{1}{4}$ = _____

7 $6\frac{4}{5}$ x $3\frac{3}{4}$ = _____

8 $7\frac{1}{3}$ x $9\frac{3}{6}$ = _____

9 $4\frac{7}{8}$ x $1\frac{1}{3}$ = _____

10 $8\frac{1}{2}$ x $2\frac{2}{3}$ = _____

Key

$22\frac{1}{2}$ .... D	$22\frac{2}{3}$ I	$4\frac{7}{24}$ .... W
$2\frac{3}{10}$ .... G	12 .... O	$25\frac{1}{2}$ .... U
$38\frac{1}{2}$ .... U	$69\frac{2}{3}$ .... R	9 .... K
$24\frac{2}{15}$ ...... T	$18\frac{1}{3}$ .... D	28 .... E
4 L	$19\frac{1}{4}$ .... A	$6\frac{1}{2}$ .... F

Riddle Answer

___ ___ ___ ___ ___   ___ ___ ___ ___ ___ **res**
7 **3** **5** **2** **8**   **9** **6** **10** **1** **4**

NAME_____ DATE_____

Riddle 35

What did the banana do when it saw the monkey?

What To Do

Solve the division problems below. Write your answers in simplest terms.
Match each answer to a letter in the Key. Then write the letter in the space above its
problem number to find the answer to the riddle.

1 $10 \div \frac{1}{2} =$ _____

2 $20 \div \frac{1}{5} =$ _____

3 $15 \div \frac{3}{5} =$ _____

4 $30 \div \frac{2}{3} =$ _____

5 $20 \div \frac{2}{5} =$ _____

6 $36 \div \frac{2}{3} =$ _____

7 $40 \div \frac{5}{10} =$ _____

8 $64 \div \frac{2}{6} =$ _____

9 $22 \div \frac{2}{3} =$ _____

10 $48 \div \frac{3}{8} =$ _____

Key

27 . . . . E	25 . . . . A	192 . . . . N
54 L	80 . . . . N	45 I
128 . . . . A	14 . . . . F	100 . . . . P
75 . . . . G	20 . . . . A	64 . . . . K
33 . . . . T	15 . . . . O	50 . . . . S

Riddle Answer

The b __ __ __ __ __   __ __ __ __ __!

NAME_____   DATE _____

Riddle 36

What do you do for a blue elephant?

What To Do

Solve the division problems below. Write your answers in simplest terms.
Match each answer to a letter in the Key. Then write the letter in the space above
its problem number to find the answer to the riddle.

1 $\dfrac{1}{2} \div \dfrac{1}{2} =$ _____

2 $\dfrac{4}{6} \div \dfrac{1}{3} =$ _____

3 $\dfrac{3}{5} \div \dfrac{1}{6} =$ _____

4 $\dfrac{9}{10} \div \dfrac{1}{5} =$ _____

5 $\dfrac{3}{5} \div \dfrac{2}{3} =$ _____

6 $\dfrac{7}{10} \div \dfrac{2}{5} =$ _____

7 $\dfrac{3}{4} \div \dfrac{1}{4} =$ _____

8 $\dfrac{5}{6} \div \dfrac{1}{8} =$ _____

9 $\dfrac{7}{9} \div \dfrac{4}{5} =$ _____

10 $\dfrac{2}{7} \div \dfrac{3}{7} =$ _____

Key

$6\,2/3$ C	$35/36$ .... E	$2/3$ .... H
3 .... U	$9/10$ .... H	1 .... E
2............ M	$4\,1/2$ I	$7/10$ .... T
$6\,3/5$ .... J	5 .... S	$4\,3/4$ .... O
$1\,1/2$ .... A	$1\,3/4$ .... R	$3\,3/5$ .... P

Riddle Answer

___ ___ ___ ___ ___   ___ ___ ___   ___ ___!
8 **5** **1** **9** **6** **10** **4** **2** **7** **3**

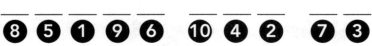

NAME _____   DATE _____

Riddle 37

What do you call a crate full of ducks?

What To Do

Solve the division problems below. Write your answers in simplest terms. Match each answer to a letter in the Key. Then write the letter in the space above its problem number to find the answer to the riddle.

1 $\dfrac{10}{12} \div \dfrac{3}{4} =$ _____

2 $\dfrac{14}{15} \div \dfrac{1}{6} =$ _____

3 $\dfrac{9}{20} \div \dfrac{7}{10} =$ _____

4 $\dfrac{7}{12} \div \dfrac{14}{25} =$ _____

5 $\dfrac{22}{30} \div \dfrac{4}{5} =$ _____

6 $\dfrac{30}{36} \div \dfrac{1}{4} =$ _____

7 $\dfrac{13}{15} \div \dfrac{2}{5} =$ _____

8 $\dfrac{24}{34} \div \dfrac{3}{8} =$ _____

9 $\dfrac{36}{42} \div \dfrac{4}{7} =$ _____

10 $\dfrac{27}{50} \div \dfrac{3}{5} =$ _____

Key

$5\,^4/_5$ .... W	$1\,^1/_9$ .... S	$1\,^{15}/_{17}$ .... F
$^{11}/_{15}$ I	$^9/_{10}$ .... A	$1\,^{31}/_{36}$ .... M
$3\,^1/_3$ .... E	$5\,^3/_5$ .... Q	$^7/_{12}$ .... D
$1\,^1/_2$ C	$2\,^1/_6$ .... U	$^9/_{14}$ .... K
$1\,^2/_9$ .... P	$1\,^1/_{24}$ .... R	$^{11}/_{12}$ .... O

Riddle Answer

A box ___ ___   ___ ___ ___ ___ ___ ___ ___ ___

NAME_____ DATE _____

Riddle 38

Where do frogs put their money?

What To Do

Solve the division problems below. Write your answers in simplest terms. Match each answer to a letter in the Key. Then write the letter in the space above its problem number to find the answer to the riddle.

1 $\frac{24}{36} \div 8 =$ _____

2 $\frac{20}{26} \div 5 =$ _____

3 $\frac{32}{41} \div 4 =$ _____

4 $\frac{28}{56} \div 2 =$ _____

5 $\frac{55}{74} \div 5 =$ _____

6 $\frac{18}{35} \div 9 =$ _____

7 $\frac{45}{58} \div 3 =$ _____

8 $\frac{75}{90} \div 3 =$ _____

9 $\frac{45}{63} \div 5 =$ _____

10 $\frac{24}{39} \div 8 =$ _____

Key

$9/43$ .... D	$1/13$ .... E	$25/57$ .... U
$2/35$ .... R	$2/13$ .... K	$5/18$ V
$1/4$ .... N	$11/74$ .... A	$1/7$ .... A
$15/58$ .... B	$17/29$ .... O	$4/53$ L
$15/31$ .... P	$8/41$ I	$1/12$ .... R

Riddle Answer

In ___ ___ ___ ___ ___ ___ ___ ___ ___ ___
⑤ ⑥ ③ ⑧ ⑩ ① ⑦ ⑨ ④ ②

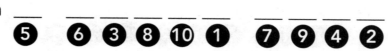

NAME_____   DATE_____

Riddle 39

Why did the spider buy a car?

What To Do

Solve the division problems below. Write your answers in simplest terms.
Match each answer to a letter in the Key. Then write the letter in the space above
its problem number to find the answer to the riddle.

❶ $7\frac{1}{8} \div 4\frac{3}{4} =$ _____

❷ $2\frac{2}{3} \div 6\frac{2}{5} =$ _____

❸ $3\frac{3}{7} \div 1\frac{1}{5} =$ _____

❹ $4\frac{1}{5} \div 6\frac{3}{10} =$ _____

❺ $5\frac{7}{8} \div 2\frac{5}{12} =$ _____

❻ $8\frac{4}{9} \div 1\frac{1}{3} =$ _____

❼ $10\frac{5}{6} \div 3\frac{6}{8} =$ _____

❽ $9\frac{4}{5} \div 4\frac{3}{15} =$ _____

❾ $15\frac{9}{10} \div 12\frac{3}{8} =$ _____

❿ $12\frac{1}{2} \div 10\frac{5}{6} =$ _____

Key

$33\,^{27}/_{32}$ ..... Y	$2\,^2/_5$ .... B	$1\,^2/_{13}$ .... A
$6\,^1/_3$ .... F	$2\,^1/_3$ I	$14\,^3/_4$ L
$17\,^1/_{15}$ ...... E	$1\,^1/_2$ .... R	$^2/_3$ I
$1\,^{47}/_{165}$ ...... O	$2\,^{25}/_{58}$ ...... N	$2\,^6/_7$ .... P
$2\,^8/_9$ .... S	$^5/_{12}$ .... T	$2\,^3/_8$ .... W

Riddle Answer

To take ___ ___ ___ ___ ___ ___ ___ ___ ___ ___
        ❽ ❷ ❻ ❾ ❶ ❿ ❼ ❸ ❹ ❺

NAME _____ DATE _____

Riddle 40

What did the ghost eat for lunch?

What To Do

Solve the problems below. Write your answers in simplest terms.
Match each answer to a letter in the Key. Then write the letter in the space above
its problem number to find the answer to the riddle.

1 There are 10 apples. Six of the apples are green. What fraction of the apples are green? _____

2 There are 20 pens. Thirteen of the pens are black. Seven of the pens are blue. What fraction of the pens are blue? _____

3 There are 12 pieces of fruit in a basket. There are 3 bananas, 5 apples, and 4 oranges. What fraction of the fruits are bananas? _____

4 There are 9 crayons. Four of the crayons are blue. Two of the crayons are yellow. Three of the crayons are red. What fraction of the crayons are not blue? _____

5 There are 11 cups. Six of the cups contain milk. One of the cups contains soda. Four of the cups contain water. What fraction of the cups contain milk and water? _____

6 There are 15 T-shirts. Twelve of the shirts are brown. What fraction of the shirts are brown? _____

7 There are 50 pairs of pants. One-half of the pants are black. One-fifth of the pants are tan. How many pairs of pants are not black or tan? _____

8 There are 36 pairs of shoes. One-third of the pairs of shoes are green. One-half of the pairs of shoes are red. How many pairs of shoes are not red or green? _____

9 There are 40 balls. One-fourth are footballs. One-tenth are soccer balls. One-half are basketballs. How many are basketballs and soccer balls? _____

10 There are 17 pictures. Eight of the pictures are of Jim. Four of the pictures are of Marla. What fraction of the pictures are of Marla? _____

Key

15	L
7	F
$5/9$	Y
$13/20$	E
24	O
8	N
$10/11$	O
$1/4$	E
$4/5$	B
12	K
$7/20$	O
$2/3$	O
$4/17$	N
$3/5$	S
6	A

Riddle Answer

___ ___ ___ ___ - ___ ___ ___ ___ ___ ___ andwich
8 **6** **9** **2** **7** **5** **10** **3** **4** **1**

Answers

Riddle 1 (page 5)
1. 4
2. 2
3. 8
4. 6
5. 12
6. 3
7. 10
8. 5
9. 7
10. 9

What should you do when two snails start fighting?
Let them slug it out.

Riddle 2 (page 6)
1. 1/2
2. 3/4
3. 3/5
4. 2/5
5. 5/8
6. 5/6
7. 4/7
8. 6/9

What did the egg do when it heard a joke?
It cracked up!

Riddle 3 (page 7)
1. 1/2
2. 1/3
3. 1/4
4. 1/6
5. 1/8
6. 1/7
7. 2/3
8. 3/4
9. 3/5
10. 2/7

What do you get from an angry shark?
As far away as possible

Riddle 4 (page 8)
1. 5/6
2. 7/11
3. 9/16
4. 5/8
5. 7/9
6. 5/14
7. 5/12
8. 12/13
9. 8/19
10. 6/15

Which dance did the chicken refuse to do?
The fox-trot

Riddle 5 (page 9)
1. 5
2. 7
3. 3
4. 10
5. 1/2
6. 3/2
7. 2 1/2
8. 5/6
9. 7/6
10. 3 1/6

Why did the monster need a third sock?
He grew another foot.

Riddle 6 (page 10)
1. 3/4
2. 3/6
3. 1/4
4. 4/5
5. 4/10
6. 5/2
7. 6/7
8. 6/25
9. 2/3
10. 1/6

Why was six scared of seven?
Because seven "ate" nine.

Riddle 7 (page 11)
1. 1/2
2. 1/4
3. 1/3
4. 1/5
5. 3/4
6. 2/3
7. 2/5
8. 3/8
9. 4/9
10. 2/7

Who won the race between the two balls of string?
They were tied.

Riddle 8 (page 12)
1. 1/2
2. 4/5
3. 4/11
4. 3/5
5. 13/32
6. 2/5
7. 9/19
8. 12/23
9. 5/7
10. 20/29

What kind of dog did the vampire own?
A bloodhound

Riddle 9 (page 13)
1. 1/3
2. 5/6
3. 12/13
4. 9/10
5. 18/22
6. 2/7
7. 1/2
8. 4/15
9. 25/70
10. 24/40

If I have 5 apples in one hand and 6 apples in the other, what would I have?
Two big hands

Riddle 10 (page 14)
1. 1 1/2
2. 1 2/3
3. 1 5/8
4. 2 1/3
5. 2 1/7
6. 7 1/5
7. 3 5/6
8. 1 3/5
9. 4 3/11
10. 1 1/3

Why is it hard to play sports against a team of big cats?
They might be cheetahs.

Riddle 11 (page 15)
1. 17/5
2. 31/4
3. 7/3
4. 3/2
5. 23/5
6. 20/3
7. 19/2
8. 35/4
9. 47/6
10. 21/4

Why did the hen run away?
She was chicken.

Riddle 12 (page 16)
1. 1
2. 1/2
3. 2/3
4. 4/5
5. 6/7
6. 5/8
7. 7/9
8. 5/6
9. 3/4
10. 4/9

What does a lion lawyer study?
The law of the jungle

Riddle 13 (page 17)
1. 1 1/3
2. 1 1/4
3. 1 2/5
4. 1 1/2
5. 1 4/9
6. 1 3/8
7. 1 1/11
8. 1 7/9
9. 1 7/15
10. 1 1/6

Where do ghosts go swimming?
The Dead Sea

Riddle 14 (page 18)
1. 1 3/5
2. 1 13/24
3. 1 13/35
4. 1 4/27
5. 1 1/18
6. 1
7. 1 7/19
8. 1 29/45
9. 1 1/4
10. 1 1/21

How do you stop a rhinoceros from charging?
Take away its credit cards.

Riddle 15 (page 19)
1. 1/4
2. 3/8
3. 2/5
4. 1/3
5. 1/5
6. 3/7
7. 1/9
8. 1/8
9. 2/7
10. 1/6

Why didn't the dog want to play ball?
It was a boxer.

Riddle 16 (page 20)
1. 2/3
2. 3/5
3. 9/20
4. 3/8
5. 3/25
6. 7/17
7. 2/5
8. 7/13
9. 1/6
10. 4/9

Where did the monster go when she lost her hand?
A second-hand shop

Riddle 17 (page 21)
1. 3
2. 4
3. 8 2/3
4. 6 2/3
5. 7 4/5
6. 10 1/7
7. 14 1/3
8. 11 1/8
9. 5 4/9
10. 6 1/8

What is big, gray, and flies straight up?
An 'elecopter

Riddle 18 (page 22)
1. 1 1/3
2. 2 2/5
3. 2 2/7
4. 3 1/2
5. 2 1/4
6. 4 3/5
7. 4 1/3
8. 3 1/6
9. 1 1/5
10. 2 4/7

Why did the tennis player hit the ball softly?
So he wouldn't make a racket.

Riddle 19 (page 23)
1. 5/6
2. 13/20
3. 11/18
4. 7/10
5. 17/35
6. 7/12
7. 1
8. 5/9
9. 9/14
10. 5/8

Why couldn't the ghost tell a lie?
You can see right through him.

Riddle 20 (page 24)
1. 1 1/4
2. 1 11/24
3. 31/35
4. 1 7/40
5. 1 4/9
6. 1 7/44
7. 29/30
8. 37/60
9. 1 3/10

10. 1 7/100
What do you get if you cross a sheepdog with a tulip?
A collie-flower

Riddle 21 (page 25)
1. 3/10
2. 1/4
3. 1/2
4. 1/5
5. 0
6. 1/24
7. 1/9
8. 3/16
9. 4/25
10. 1/21
What did the orangutan call his wife?
His prime-mate

Riddle 22 (page 26)
1. 5/21
2. 1/8
3. 17/44
4. 5/24
5. 17/30
6. 11/120
7. 1/18
8. 1/10
9. 1/5
10. 7/24
What do you say when you meet a two-headed dragon?
"Hello! Hello!"

Riddle 23 (page 27)
1. 7/40
2. 37/44
3. 3/26
4. 8/9
5. 11/30
6. 1
7. 55/96
8. 31/40
9. 2/5
10. 35/36
What did one keyboard say to another keyboard?
"You are my type."

Riddle 24 (page 28)
1. 6 3/4
2. 7 1/2
3. 11 5/6
4. 4 7/8
5. 11 23/36
6. 11 1/15
7. 7 5/7
8. 6 7/15
9. 16 5/8
10. 12 17/18
What do frogs say when they meet each other?
"Warts new with you?"

Riddle 25 (page 29)
1. 2 1/4
2. 3 1/8
3. 2 1/3
4. 4 1/8
5. 5 5/12
6. 3 4/15
7. 6 4/35
8. 4 1/30
9. 11 3/44
10. 7 2/9
What kind of horse always looks fashionable?
A clotheshorse

Riddle 26 (page 30)
1. 0.8
2. 0.75
3. 0.5
4. 0.6
5. 0.25
6. 0.125
7. 0.375
8. 0.4
9. 0.625
10. 0.9
What did the hot dog say to the hamburger?
"Nice to meat you!"

Riddle 27 (page 31)
1. 2.5
2. 4.25
3. 1.6
4. 7.2
5. 5.25
6. 11.2
7. 3.25
8. 9.5

9. 5.8
10. 7.1
If you had 10 cows and 10 goats, what would you have?
Lots of milk

Riddle 28 (page 32)
1. 1/2
2. 0.75
3. 2 1/2
4. 3 2/3
5. 4 1/2
6. 0.04
7. 0.032
8. 16/8
9. 2.96
10. 5 1/6
When is the best time to tell a joke?
In the laughter-noon

Riddle 29 (page 33)
1. 1/4
2. 11/16
3. 2/5
4. 3/5
5. 6/7
6. 14/33
7. 2/3
8. 2/23
9. 4/5
10. 8/11
What is a baby elephant after she is eight weeks old?
Nine weeks old

Riddle 30 (page 34)
1. 1/6
2. 3/28
3. 3/20
4. 8/21
5. 5/48
6. 1/9
7. 3/14
8. 1/4
9. 2/5
10. 15/56
What is a frog's favorite shoe?
An open-toad sandal

Riddle 31 (page 35)
1. 1/3
2. 10/21
3. 27/40
4. 16/21
5. 8/25
6. 7/24
7. 36/77
8. 7/36
9. 5/12
10. 5/8

What did the elephant say when his tail was grabbed?
"That's the end of me!"

Riddle 32 (page 36)
1. 1
2. 4
3. 1 4/5
4. 1 1/3
5. 5/7
6. 3
7. 3 8/9
8. 1 3/5
9. 2 5/11
10. 5

How do squirrels feel when you hide their food?
It drives them nuts!

Riddle 33 (page 37)
1. 2 1/2
2. 2 3/4
3. 3 3/8
4. 1 4/5
5. 1 9/10
6. 5 1/2
7. 4
8. 2
9. 6
10. 4 1/5

Why were the elephants asked to leave the swimming pool?
They couldn't keep their trunks up.

Riddle 34 (page 38)
1. 4
2. 28
3. 18 1/3
4. 38 1/2
5. 22 1/2
6. 19 1/4
7. 25 1/2
8. 69 2/3
9. 6 1/2
10. 22 2/3

What do you call cows that can't produce milk?
Udder failures

Riddle 35 (page 39)
1. 20
2. 100
3. 25
4. 45
5. 50
6. 54
7. 80
8. 192
9. 33
10. 128

What did the banana do when it saw the monkey?
The banana split!

Riddle 36 (page 40)
1. 1
2. 2
3. 3 3/5
4. 4 1/2
5. 9/10
6. 1 3/4
7. 3
8. 6 2/3
9. 35/36
10. 2/3

What do you do for a blue elephant?
Cheer him up!

Riddle 37 (page 41)
1. 1 1/9
2. 5 3/5
3. 9/14
4. 1 1/24
5. 11/12
6. 3 1/3
7. 2 1/6
8. 1 15/17

9. 1 1/2
10. 9/10

What do you call a crate full of ducks?
A box of quackers

Riddle 38 (page 42)
1. 1/12
2. 2/13
3. 8/41
4. 1/4
5. 11/74
6. 2/35
7. 15/58
8. 5/18
9. 1/7
10. 1/13

Where do frogs put their money?
In a river bank

Riddle 39 (page 43)
1. 1 1/2
2. 5/12
3. 2 6/7
4. 2/3
5. 2 25/58
6. 6 1/3
7. 2 8/9
8. 2 1/3
9. 1 47/165
10. 1 2/13

Why did the spider buy a car?
To take it for a spin

Riddle 40 (page 44)
1. 3/5
2. 7/20
3. 1/4
4. 5/9
5. 10/11
6. 4/5
7. 15
8. 6
9. 24
10. 4/17

What did the ghost eat for lunch?
A boo-loney sandwich